Edouard Naville

The Temple of Deir el Bahari

Edouard Naville

The Temple of Deir el Bahari

ISBN/EAN: 9783337803049

Printed in Europe, USA, Canada, Australia, Japan

Cover: Foto ©Thomas Meinert / pixelio.de

More available books at **www.hansebooks.com**

THE TEMPLE OF

DEIR EL BAHARI:

ITS PLAN, ITS FOUNDERS, AND ITS FIRST EXPLORERS.

INTRODUCTORY MEMOIR

BY

EDOUARD NAVILLE, D.Litt., D.Phil.,

CORRESPONDENT OF THE INSTITUTE OF FRANCE; HONORARY FELLOW OF KING'S COLLEGE, LONDON.

TWELFTH MEMOIR OF

THE EGYPT EXPLORATION FUND.

PUBLISHED BY ORDER OF THE COMMITTEE.

LONDON:
SOLD AT
THE OFFICES OF THE EGYPT EXPLORATION FUND, 37, GREAT RUSSELL STREET, W.C.,
AND 15, BLAGDEN STREET, BOSTON, MASS., U.S.A.;
AND BY KEGAN PAUL, TRENCH, TRÜBNER & CO., PATERNOSTER HOUSE, CHARING CROSS ROAD;
B. QUARITCH, 15, PICCADILLY; A. ASHER & CO., 13, BEDFORD STREET, COVENT GARDEN.

1891.

EGYPT EXPLORATION FUND.

PREFACE.

THIS Memoir is not intended to be a full statement of the results hitherto obtained from the present excavations at Deir el Bahari, but simply as an introductory volume describing the building, its plan, and the period to which it belongs, and also giving an account of the work accomplished by previous excavators on this spot, and especially by Mariette. I have dwelt at some length on the reign of Hatshepsu, whose temple of Deir el Bahari was at once her own creation and her noblest monument.

Some reference to discoveries made in the course of the last two winters' excavations was unavoidable, and I have more than once alluded to them, particularly in showing how they have corrected erroneous restorations of the plan of the building. But I have carefully refrained from drawing from these discoveries any premature inferences which might have to be modified as the work progresses. As long as the excavations are still in progress, it is not possible, on many points, to arrive at definite conclusions.

Plates Nos. I.—III. are reproductions of the plans made by the French expedition, by Lepsius, and by Mariette, and it is interesting to compare the differences between them. Lepsius' plan (Pl. II.) is evidently conjectural in places, as, for example, in the restoration of the northern part of the lower colonnade, which he cannot have seen and must have supposed to be similar to the southern part.

The phototypes contained in this volume, like those in my preceding memoirs, have been executed by the firm of MM. Thévoz et Cie, of Geneva. All the smaller illustrations are from photographs taken by Mr. Howard Carter, one of the artists attached to our staff at Deir el Bahari.

The original text of this memoir was written in French, and has been translated under the direction of the Committee.

EDOUARD NAVILLE.

Malagny,

August, 1894.

CONTENTS.

DEIR EL BAHARI.

CHAPTER I.

THE tourists who annually swarm into Thebes seldom depart from the ancient city of Amon without visiting the magnificent natural amphitheatre of Deir el Bahari, where the hills of the Libyan range present their most imposing aspect. Leaving the plain by a narrow gorge, whose walls of naked rock are honeycombed with tombs, the traveller emerges into a wide open space bounded at its further end by a semi-circular wall of cliffs. These cliffs of white limestone, which time and sun have coloured rosy yellow, form an absolutely vertical barrier. They are accessible only from the north by a steep and difficult path leading to the summit of the ridge that divides Deir el Bahari from the wild and desolate Valley of the Tombs of the Kings.

Built against these cliffs, and even as it were rooted into their sides by subterranean chambers, is the temple of which Mariette said that "it is an exception and an accident in the architectural life of Egypt."

Our earliest detailed description of the place is that given by Jollois and Devilliers, two scholars attached to the French expedition of 1798. They made a plan of what they found there, and that plan is here reproduced (pl. i.). Their description is interesting[1]; it gives us a fairly good idea of the

building as seen at the close of the last century. We can follow in the works of Wilkinson, Lepsius, and Mariette the subsequent study and exploration of the temple, the various excavations that have been made there, and also the injuries which it has sustained since its ancient ruins were in part laid bare.

The following is a summary of what we learn from the two French writers. The approach from the plain was by an avenue of sphinxes. This avenue was thirteen metres (42 feet) wide, and four hundred metres (437 yards) long, without counting a break of fifty metres (54 yards). On either side were small heaps of rubbish, symmetrically placed at regular intervals. Their original forms were not easily to be discovered at a first glance ; but any one accustomed to such ruins, like the authors of this description, would quickly recognize in these heaps the remains of pedestals for sphinxes or rams such as are still to be seen in great numbers at Karnak and at Luxor. At the western extremity of this avenue were the *débris* of two constructions, which might have formed the towers of a pylon, the entrance through the enclosure wall of the temple was made at this point. Mariette agrees with his predecessors in placing a pylon here, although nothing but its site was discernible in his time.

Still keeping to Jollois and Devilliers, and

[1] *Description de l'Égypte*, vol. ii., p. 340, Panckoucke's edition.

B

following the continuation of the avenue, we find on the north traces of a wall more than forty-five metres (49 yards) long. At each end of it are the remains of a column, but "they do not rise above the level of the ground." Here, Mariette's plan is blank (pl. iii.). These vestiges of a wall must have belonged to an adjunct of what he calls "the Eastern Terrace." Farther on we come to the ruins of two flights of steps which led up to buildings on a higher level. This description clearly applies to the avenue which is in a line with the axis of the temple. At the far end of that avenue is a rectangular edifice built on still higher ground, "forty-eight metres (52 yards) long, by twenty-nine (31 yards) wide. In the same direction lie some inner rooms whose forms are easily followed. Pococke, who saw the ruins which we describe, here found many remains of mummies. A red granite door-way, in almost perfect preservation, forms the entrance to this part of the building, and is covered with hieroglyphs in sunk relief of the most careful workmanship. It is hidden under plaster, with which it would seem to have been coated by the Christians, for images of their saints may yet be seen upon it."

There can be no doubt that the description here refers to the central part of the western platform, the highest part of the temple, and built against the rock itself. We gather that the southern chambers of the platform, which were afterwards cleared by Mariette, were not altogether buried out of sight at the close of the last century, but probably were filled with rubbish up to a certain height. Neither do I think that the floor or pavement of the platform could then be seen. The platform was reached through the granite portal, which early Christians had coated with white plaster and painted with figures of saints, and the mention of the state of this doorway and of the sanctuary by Jollois and Devilliers is the only indication given by those authors as to the later use to which the temple was put. The name of Deir el Bahari—"Convent of the North "—was apparently unknown to them, as also the fact that the temple became a convent; they never notice the Coptic superstructures, whose ruins are still standing and must then have been far more extensive. They give a long description of what is now thought to be the sanctuary, the subterranean chamber opening on to the court, to which the prolonged avenue leads. They make the chamber thirteen and a half metres (44 ft.) long, by five (16 ft.) wide. They also speak of its rounded ceiling, which is vaulted in appearance only, for we can easily see that its horizontal courses of stone were laid so as to overlap each other and finally close the space which was to be covered in, while its cylindrical form was subsequently produced by chiselling away the angles and thus shaping the ceiling into a vault of the desired curve. The sculptures of the chamber are covered with a coating of plaster painted with figures of Christ, "and this would lead us to infer that it was a place of Christian worship during the earlier centuries of our era."

Hence all that was to be seen of the temple at the close of the last century were the remains of the dromos at the entrance, and the pedestals of the sphinxes which lined it on either side. The two first platforms must have been completely covered with sand except for the outcrop of certain lengths of wall on the north side of the lower, or eastern platform; but further, the central part of the upper platform was visible, and the subterranean chamber was also accessible. Traces of long-abandoned Christian worship remained upon all that was then found standing. The general appearance of the site was much the same earlier in the century; for Pococke, who visited the spot in 1737, and is quoted by Jollois and Devilliers, gives a similar account to theirs. His description is very short, and by no means clear. After mentioning the mummies—which abounded—he adds that "here it seemed as though the mountain had been vertically hewn out by the hand of man, and the people of the place said that there had once been a passage through it into the next valley."

Champollion and Wilkinson must have visited Deïr el Bahari within a short interval one of the other. Champollion' scarcely pauses to describe the building, which seems to have been in much the same condition as it was in the days of Jollois and Devilliers. He tells us that his object in going to study it was " to fix the as yet unknown date of the edifice, and to ascertain its original purpose." He was chiefly attracted by the upper part, and the granite portal leading to it, on which he read the cartouche of Thothmes III., "called Mœris by the Greeks." He at once perceived that the cartouches of Thothmes III. were usurpations, and that they must have superseded two others, which were all the more readily determined since he found them upon the temple walls. The second of these cartouches—that of Queen Hatshepsu—he read *Amenenthe*,[2] but declined to call it a queen's. He persists in regarding it as belonging to a king, and hence offers no satisfactory explanation of the employment of the feminine form in all the inscriptions. "If," says he, " I felt somewhat surprised at seeing here, as elsewhere throughout the temple, the renowned Mœris, adorned with all the insignia of royalty, giving place to this Amenenthe, for whose name we may search the royal lists in vain, still more astonished was I to find on reading the inscriptions that wherever they referred to this bearded king in the usual dress of the Pharaohs, nouns and verbs were in the feminine, as though a queen were in question. I found the same peculiarity everywhere. Not only was there the prenomen of Amenenthe preceded by the title of sovereign ruler of the world, *with the feminine affix*, but also his own name immediately following on the title of ' daughter of the Sun.' Finally, in all the bas-reliefs representing the gods speaking to this king, he is addressed as a queen, as in the following formula: ' Behold, thus saith Amon-Ra, lord of the thrones of the world, to his daughter whom he loves, sun devoted to the truth : the building which thou hast made is like to the divine dwelling.'"

By way of solving this problem, Champollion propounded the existence of a queen called *Amense*, sister of Thothmes II. He thought to have found her name in a cartouche attached to that of an unknown Thothmes, who would have been her first husband, and who must have reigned in his wife's name. On his death, Amense must have taken Amenenthe for her second husband, and he also ruled in her name. She evidently predeceased him, for Amenenthe afterwards reigned conjointly with Thothmes III., "the Mœris of the Greeks," who was under his guardianship. The ward would not seem to have felt much gratitude towards his guardian, but did his utmost to consign him to oblivion, by diligently hammering out his legends.

Champollion proved from the inscriptions that the temple was dedicated to Amon. According to several travellers who had preceded him, this edifice with " vaulted " ceilings could be no other than the tomb of Mœris ; but its chambers and accessories show it to be a genuine temple, for they contain scenes of offerings to the gods and to the ancestors of the Pharaohs. Champollion notes signs of restorations by Horus, Rameses the Great, his son Merenphtah, and later by Ptolemy Euergetes II. Remarking on the inferiority of sculptures of the Greek period as compared with the magnificent bas-reliefs of the XVIIIth Dynasty, Champollion takes the opportunity of giving renewed expression to one of his favourite ideas, viz : that, far from having profited by Greek influence, Egyptian art had only suffered through it. It was his conviction that the origin of Greek art lay in servile imitation of the Egyptian. Ancient Egypt had taught her arts to Greece, who developed them to the point of sublimity ; but had it not been for Egypt,

---

[1] *Lettres écrites d'Égypte et de Nubie*, no. 15.

[2] The cartouche is read *Amonenhe* in the *Notices*.

Greece would in all probability never have become the classic land of the fine arts.

In 1827 Wilkinson was in the temple, since he speaks of excavations which he then made, for the purpose of clearing part of the walls.[1] He calls the building by the same name under which it is known to us:—"Below the cliffs of the Libyan mountain is an ancient temple, whose modern name, Dayr el Bahri, or the northern convent, indicates its having served, like the vicinity and precincts of most of the temples of Thebes, as a church and monastery of the early Christians." He speaks of the long dromos leading, between two rows of sphinxes whose fragments still remain, to a square enclosure before which two pedestals mark the sites of two obelisks. Wilkinson's description is somewhat confused. He mentions an inclined plane of masonry leading to the central court of the temple, and intersecting at right angles a covered corridor formed by a peristyle of eight polygonal columns. "The inner face of this corridor, which is the front of the first scarp of a series of terraces," is doubtless what Mariette called the "Eastern Terrace." Wilkinson gives us some interesting details as to the sculptures adorning its walls. On the southern side are processions of soldiers carrying boughs or weapons, the sacrifice of an ox, and the remains of two boats. All this may still be seen, and even more than Wilkinson describes. A scene found by the English traveller, and representing the dedication of two obelisks to Amon by the royal founder of the temple, has not altogether disappeared, though it has considerably suffered. These obelisks, very different from those of Diospolis (Karnak), must have been erected on the pedestals at the end of the dromos. Wilkinson translates the accompanying inscription. After giving the names and titles of the Pharaoh Amunneitgori,[2] the inscription goes on to say:

[1] *Topography of Thebes*, 1835 edition, p. 90.

[2] See the description in Murray's *Handbook*, 1867 ed., of which the bulk is derived from Wilkinson. The name of the Pharaoh is there read *Amun noo-het*, instead of *Amunneitgori*.

" she has made (this) her work for her father Amunre, lord of the regions (and) erected to him two fine obelisks of granite . . . . . she did this (who is) the giver of life like the sun for ever."

This bas-relief supplies evidence in favour of Wilkinson's theory that there were two obelisks at the entrance to the temple. It also seems to furnish an indication that the blocks which were found built into walls erected on the upper platform carved with scenes referring to the transport of two obelisks—in one case showing one of the monuments placed upon a sledge — had been brought thither from the eastern platform by the Copts.

Coming to the granite gateway which gives access to the western platform, Wilkinson, like Champollion, testifies that its inscription is in the feminine, and refers to the Pharaoh whose name he reads as Amunneitgori ; all the same, he hesitates to call this sovereign a queen. He describes the bas-reliefs, and in this connection confutes Champollion's hypothesis of a queen Amense, wife to an unknown Thothmes. He proves that the unknown Thothmes is no other than Thothmes II., and that there was no queen Amense. He also mentions the tradition of the existence of a passage connecting the temple of Deir el Bahari with the valley of Biban el Molouk.

Whether any one worked at Deir el Bahari after Champollion we do not know ; but certainly Lepsius appears to have seen something more of the temple than his predecessors, as may be gathered from his plan of the building (pl. ii.). He describes the dromos (but without speaking of any obelisks), the western platform, the granite gateway, and the sanctuary. Lepsius believes that the temple was originally connected with that of Karnak, since the axis of the prolonged dromos would lead straight to the great temple of Amon. He was the first to discover the founder of the temple, which he still calls the temple of the Assassif. It was a queen, *Numt Amen*, eldest sister of Thothmes III., who devised this bold scheme for uniting the two sides of the Nile valley. She it was who erected before the temple of Karnak the two largest obelisks left to us. *Numt Amen* are the two first words of the cartouche of Hatshepsu, and Lepsius had in truth recognised the name of the founder of the temple, although, as he had at once observed, the queen is never represented as a woman, but always in the dress of a man. Her sex is revealed by the inscriptions. "Doubtless it was contrary to the law of succession for a queen to occupy the throne, and this was the reason that her brother, probably still a minor, subsequently appears as sharing the throne along with her. After the queen's death her cartouches were replaced by those of Thuthmosis III., and her name was not admitted upon the lists of legitimate sovereigns."[1]

[1] *Brie,* p. 282.

CHAPTER II.

MARIETTE.

From the days of Lepsius onwards, hunters after mummies and antiquities have probably attacked Deir el Bahari from time to time. Of this I had a proof on the 14th February 1893, when, on reaching the roof of the covered chamber situate at the N.W. angle of the western platform—a chamber unknown to Mariette—I found a pencilled notice on its walls stating that it had been opened by Greene in 1855.

Mariette made three excavations at Deir el Bahari, but regrets having been unable to work there as uninterruptedly as in other parts of Egypt. "On three occasions only (1858, 1862, 1866) was I able to take small detachments of men from the excavations at Goornah and make more or less successful attempts on Deir el Bahari." The first proved to be the most important in its results. Then it was that the plan of the temple was ascertained (pl. iii.), and discovery made of the famous bas-reliefs of the naval expedition to the land of Punt. The subsequent explorations chiefly served to form collections of sarcophagi and mummies, either for the Museum of Boulaq or for the Paris Universal Exhibition of 1867.

Deir el Bahari—the Convent of the North, which the people of the place also call Deir el Assassif—the Convent of the Assassif—or Deir es Sultan—the Convent of the King—bears that name because ruins of a Coptic convent stand on part of the temple site even to this day. The Copts did not take possession of the whole; they did not occupy the eastern platform. But it was from this platform that they took material for building the wretched walls which divided their convent into different rooms. These walls are either of brick, brick and stone, or altogether of stone. The latter are built of miscellaneous sculptured blocks, capitals and bases of columns being used indiscriminately with bas-reliefs turned upside down. The destruction and the havoc wrought in this temple by the Copts is incalculable. For instance, all the great wall at the end of the western platform, built against the rock, and protecting the court on the west, is made of ancient blocks. Mariette did not see this wall. In the course of my first winter's work I cleared a good deal of it, and satisfied myself that it contains fragments of very important inscriptions which must, if possible, be completed as the excavation proceeds.

Mariette rightly insisted upon the peculiar character of the temples on the left bank of the river at Thebes. Here only do we find a certain special type of building, and all the examples date from the comparatively limited period covered by the XVIIIth to the XXth Dynasties. The great temples on the right bank of the Nile—Karnak, Luxor—are in the first place buildings erected for the worship of the local deity, and the work of many generations. From the time of the XIIth Dynasty, the dynasty of the Amenemhats and Usertesens, almost every sovereign or reigning family undertook the duty of adding to or repairing the structure of Karnak. Each generation insisted on being represented there, so that the walls of the great temple of Amon became as it were the annals of the Egyptian monarchy. It is altogether otherwise with the temples on the left bank. There the king began a temple with the intention of completing it himself. The plan was his, and he tried to carry it out from beginning to end; for, in fact, these temples were monuments raised by the king to his own glory and to his own memory, and the inscriptions with which they are covered often take the form of chapters from his autobiography. In order to understand the object of these temples we must compare them with the Egyptian tomb such as it was even under the Old Kingdom. An Egyptian tomb consisted of three parts: the exterior chapel, the shaft, and the sepulchral chamber. The exterior chapel was composed of one or more rooms, sometimes lavishly decorated, adorned with colonnades or peristyles, and always accessible to the kindred of the deceased and to his priests, if he had any. Hither came his family to make libations and bring offerings of food and incense to the dead: they also came at certain times in the year to celebrate religious rites, whose nature and details were prescribed by the ceremonial code.

In the chapel, or near to it, was the opening of the vertical shaft by which the sarcophagus was introduced into the sepulchral chamber. This pit was filled up, and the chamber hermetically closed, so that no one could gain access to the mummy, which must be secured from sight, and above all from sacrilege. The funerary chapel, on the other hand, was open to visitors, and there the dead man wished to show what his life had been. As may be seen at Beni Hassan, it was here that he had caused his praises to be inscribed, and that it had pleased him to set forth to posterity the rare qualities by which he had been distinguished, the high deeds which had marked his career, the dignities to which the royal favour had raised him, and the riches that he had gathered.

Let us now return to Thebes, to the entrance of the vast necropolis which occupies so large a space on the left bank of the river, and consider the tombs destined for the greatest personages in the realm, that is to say for the kings. Here we find the three essential parts of the Ancient and Middle Kingdom tomb, but instead of being all together, or at least in close proximity

to each other, they are separated by considerable distances. In the Valley of the Kings, far from cultivated land, and in the midst of a solitude that one is little tempted to disturb, is the sepulchral chamber, and the equivalent of the shaft, namely the long subterranean gallery penetrating far into the rock, and often excavated at several different levels. None of this was meant to be accessible, and all was hermetically closed. Outside the valley, and nearer to the town, standing out against the sand of the desert in sight of all men, and close to a college of priests, was the chapel to which offerings were brought, and where rites were celebrated through the pious care of the family, or of visitors. But the chapel had grown into a temple; of such temples there must once have been several, and four of them are standing to this day: Goornah, the Ramesseum, Medinet Haboo and Deir el Bahari.

It is to Mariette that we must give the credit of having fully recognised the nature and function of these temples of the left bank. They are great funerary chapels, closely connected with the royal tombs whose existence they imply. Their special character being determined, we may now proceed to divide these funerary temples into two categories: those erected for a single sovereign, and those which were intended to serve for several royal tombs. To the first category belong the Ramesseum and Medinet Haboo. Rameses II., the vainest and most ostentatious of Egyptian kings, and after him that one among his successors who, dazzled by the external magnificence and vainglory of his reign, seems to have resolved to imitate him in every way— Rameses III.—built their own funerary chapels, monuments designed to perpetuate their mighty deeds, and to carry down to posterity what they esteemed as their chief titles to fame. Hence each of these temples was in connection with one tomb only. It was otherwise with those of Goornah and Deir el Bahari. Seti I. began the building at Goornah, and there raised a funerary chapel to his father, Rameses I. The inscriptions on the walls show that Rameses was dead, and he is represented as seated in his sanctuary and bearing the emblems of Osiris. In his honour the temple was built and the ceremonies celebrated. Seti I. did not complete the building. Rameses II. continued it, and adhering to its original dedication consecrated it also to his father, Seti I.; for in a large bas-relief we see Seti I. coming forth from his tomb, and invoking Amon in favour of his son, who stands before him, offering perfumes to the sacred bark of the god. The temple of Goornah is therefore the great chapel of two tombs, and it is as though in a mastabat of the Old Kingdom, or in one of the tombs of Beni Hassan, there were two pits opening from the same room.

This is also the case at Deir el Bahari. That temple belonged to several tombs whose sites are unknown to us, but which may well have been in its immediate neighbourhood. Mariette thought that the queen had built it with regard to her own tomb only; but had he made further excavations in the direction of the north-west angle of the western platform, which I cleared last spring, he would have seen that the building, although certainly made for the queen, was in the first place intended to be the funerary temple of her father, Thothmes I. The rock-cut chapel of that king, which I discovered, and the altar placed before its door, seem to show that the queen's first thought had been for Thothmes I. She chose a site which had served as a necropolis in times that were ancient even in her days, for Mariette states that at the far end of the amphitheatre, towards the south-west, there was another edifice, now utterly destroyed, which dated from King Mentuhotep II., of the

XIth Dynasty. There may even be traces of a third building of the same kind.

The temple must also have been intended for ceremonies connected with the tomb of the queen. The great vaulted chamber on the south, which was cleared by Mariette, and where we see long processions of priests bearing offerings (pl. vi.), is likewise of a funerary character. It is certain that the queen must have made her tomb in Thebes, near to the burial-places of the rest of her family, and on that side of the river where this temple stands. But where did she cause that tomb to be hewn out whose site we have never yet discovered? Is it in the valley of Biban el Molouk together with most of the royal tombs; is it peradventure in the western valley; or in some secret place beneath the walls of the temple that we are now excavating? We do not know. Did the vengeance of Thothmes III., the fury with which he erased the inscriptions of his aunt and guardian, lead him to destroy her tomb also and to cast her ashes to the wind? That is scarcely likely. The fact remains that we have the bodies of Thothmes II., Thothmes III., and according to M. Maspero, of Thothmes I., without counting those of many princes and princesses of the family—but not the body of the queen. Moreover, we do not know the tomb of any Thothmes, nor from what places or caves their mummies were removed to the hiding-place which was so well concealed as to keep the secret of its precious deposit until our time. One thing at least is certain that in Deir el Bahari we have a building which was the funerary chapel of Thothmes I. and of his daughter. Perhaps it also belonged to Thothmes II., and Thothmes III.; but of this we cannot be sure at the present stage of our researches.

THE funerary temple built by Queen Hatshepsu on the site of an XIth Dynasty necropolis bore no resemblance to other Egyptian temples ; it was *sui generis* (pl. iii.). We shall proceed to describe its plan, mainly basing our description upon the researches of Mariette. His work notwithstanding our knowledge of the temple is as yet imperfect, and it is hoped that further and complete information on the subject may result from the present excavations, which will doubtless occupy several winters. The excavations of 1893 showed

No one can fail to admire the indomitable energy and perseverance by which he triumphed over all obstacles—sometimes wantonly placed in his path—during his search for the Serapeum at the outset of his Egyptian career. But in many cases we are constrained to admit that, by his method of work, Mariette prevented himself from completing his own excavations, and made the undertaking exceedingly difficult for his successors. At Deir el Bahari he carried out on a large scale his custom of heaping his rubbish close to the place

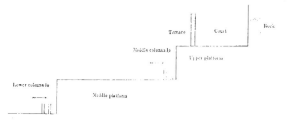

Mariette's theoretical reconstruction of the building to be inaccurate as regards the upper platform : and from time to time our own ideas of the temple will probably be modified as we clear away the mounds of rubbish still covering parts of it.

Far be it from us to detract from the merit and value of Mariette's researches, which amended and restored large portions of Egyptian history.

from which it came, instead of removing it to a distance. Probably this practice was forced upon him by circumstances, but it sometimes resulted in his covering important sites with earth or sand, and thus led to his overlooking discoveries to which he himself would have attached high value. It has several times fallen to my lot to deal with these results of Mariette's method, especially during my excavations at Deir el Bahari. In clearing the north-west corner of the upper platform, and trying to find the rock against

---

[1] The above plan gives the nomenclature which will be adopted in this and the subsequent volumes in describing the various parts of the temple at Deir el Bahari.

which that platform stands, I have not only removed the débris which concealed it from the eyes of Wilkinson and Lepsius, but I was in the first place obliged to carry away beyond the temple enclosure large accumulations from the south side of the same platform, cast here by Mariette. He had never suspected that beneath his rubbish heaps lay a hall decorated with gigantic sculptures, although Greene had noticed the top of it. Still less did he suspect that here too was the roofed chapel of Thothmes I., and an inner court containing that great altar whose discovery was the most important result of my first season's work. All this part of the temple I have completely cleared.

We must not be too severe in our judgment of Mariette; probably he would gladly have acted otherwise; but the necessity for proceeding rapidly, and the pecuniary conditions by which he was hampered all his life, obliged him to work as economically as possible. The excavator is almost invariably confronted with the difficulty of disposing of his rubbish, especially in such a place as Deir el Bahari, where the temple is shut in between hill and necropolis. Here the débris must be carried out to an old clay pit, a sort of pond which the Arabs call the lake—" birket "—in order to run no risk of covering either building or tombs.

The enclosure wall has almost entirely disappeared, but its course can still be traced. According to Mariette it embraced not only the XVIIIth Dynasty building, but also a much older funerary temple dating from the XIth Dynasty. The whole surrounding country is indeed one vast necropolis, and mummy-pits dug all over the temple of Hatshepsu show that from the time of the XXIInd Dynasty the building itself had served as a receptacle for mummies.

Not one stone is now standing of that entrance gateway near which Wilkinson found traces of a pylon. Mariette saw no objection to admitting that there had been a pylon here, but he was less willing to admit that two obelisks stood in front of it; for obelisks were not usually placed before

temples on the left bank of the river. Still, he ultimately decided that the bas-relief described by Wilkinson settled the question, and last year's excavations seem to me to confirm his opinion that two great monoliths had once adorned the entrance to the temple. Following the avenue which divides the whole length of the temple, at about 50 metres (55 yards) within the enclosure wall, Mariette notes two angles of a rectangular construction whose nature cannot be determined. Beyond it begins the graduated incline leading to that raised colonnade of the first platform, which Mariette calls the " Eastern Terrace." We shall return later to the bas-reliefs on its wall, which were protected by a roof doubly supported on a row of quadrangular pillars and another row of columns of a composite style ; the inner row being of the style sometimes called proto-Doric and found elsewhere throughout the temple. The north part of the wall is far more damaged than the south part, its bas-reliefs representing religious scenes having been almost entirely effaced. The damage at the south end has been chiefly effected by excavations in search of the many mummies found there, these excavations having also involved the removal of the pavement.

A high retaining wall, upholding the whole length of the middle platform above the valley, starts from the south-east angle of the lower or eastern platform, and is in good preservation. Its lower courses are decorated by a series of carved panellings, surmounted by alternating hawks and uræi of colossal size (pl. xiv.). This ornamentation extends the whole length of the platform, i.e., for about 90 metres (98 yards). Little remains of the pavement ; on the south it has almost entirely disappeared, owing to graves having been dug there and afterwards rifled. No complete plan of the building is possible until the great mounds of rubbish on the north side of this platform have been completely cleared away.

A graduated incline, or flight of steps, led from the centre of this platform to the upper or western platform, which was upheld by the retaining wall terminating the middle platform, just as the middle platform was upheld above the lower one. The face of this wall bears very important inscriptions, and was protected by a portico formed of two rows of square pillars. The southern half is covered with the famous pictorial representation of the expedition to the Land of Punt; on the northern half, which I have already partly cleared, are most interesting texts and scenes relating to the birth of the queen and her enthronement by her father, Thothmes I.

On the same level as the portico, and at either end of it are rock-cut sanctuaries. That on the north consists of one small central chamber parallel to the axis of the temple, opening on two others which are at right angles to each other. These three chambers are approached through a twelve-columned portico, whose roof is in perfect preservation. The scenes painted on the walls of the Northern Speos are exclusively religious; they are only partially effaced, and are full of life and colour. The Southern or Hathor Speos is the more important. It is entered through a covered vestibule whose pillars have Hathor-headed capitals, and whose walls bear scenes relating to the rejoicings at Thebes on the successful return of the fleet from the Land of Punt. On an inner wall of the Speos, Hathor is represented under the form of a cow suckling a boy bearing the queen's name.

The upper platform was occupied by various buildings. In the first place there is a terrace, and, judging by what I found on the north side, this terrace was roofed in, and the roof rested upon a single row of columns and abutted against a thick wall, now more than half ruined, on which the Copts erected their convent tower. The red granite gateway, which is exactly opposite to the entrance to the sanctuary, leads through the wall into a large inner court. This portal was seen by Jollois and Devilliers in the last century; it consists of red granite monolithic posts and lintel, and furnishes two instances of that deface-

ment of inscriptions from which the whole temple has suffered. First the queen's cartouche was chiselled out and replaced by that of her nephew, Thothmes III., who left all the rest of the inscription in the feminine : *Menkheperra* (Thothmes III.), *she has raised this monument to her father, Amon Ra.* Subsequently the name of the god was also struck out, evidently by order of Khuenaten, who, in his passionate antagonism to the worship of Amon, erased the name and figure of that divinity throughout the temple. Name and figure were afterwards roughly and imperfectly restored, and the credit of these very inferior restorations is probably due to Rameses II., who thus acquired the right of inscribing his own name on almost every wall of the temple. There is no inscription of a few yards long which does not prove to contain the following :

King Rameses II. restored these monuments of his father, Amon Ra. This formula occurs no less than five times on the south half of the wall of the lower colonnade.

Passing through the granite gateway we enter a rectangular space bounded by thick walls on the north and south, and terminated on the west by the vertical cliff which closes in the valley. This court was all that was seen by Jollois and Devilliers. Directly opposite the granite gateway, and in a line with the avenue of approach, is the rock-cut sanctuary whose "vaulted" roof, described by the French savants, is constructed in true Egyptian fashion as above explained (p. 2). The west wall of the court is a retaining wall built against the cliff side, and containing niches for offerings or sacred emblems. I cleared almost the whole of the northern half of this wall last year, and found that it had been rebuilt by the Copts, and that the blocks which they had used for this purpose are carved with fragments of a great inscription, to whose sculptures they had paid no regard whatever. The loss of this great inscription is lamentable.

Before my excavations were begun in 1893 the south side only of the upper platform had been cleared; high mounds of rubbish covered it on the north. But although the south side alone was laid bare by Mariette, and the north side invisible to him, his plan shows the wall which bounded the inner court on the north. On the south he had found several chambers, and especially one large "vaulted" room, oriented from east to west like the temple, and containing at its far end a granite stela whose inscription is completely effaced. The walls of this chamber are sculptured with processions of priests bringing offerings to Queen Hatshepsu, the work being of remarkable fineness (pl. vi.). None of these have been hammered out excepting the name of the queen.

In Mariette's, or rather M. Brune's, conjectural restoration of the upper or western platform, it is assumed that the buildings on its north side exactly correspond with those on its south. My excavations have proved that this is not the case. There are two doors in the north wall of the court. The larger and western door opens on to a somewhat high and narrow hall, lying north and south, and decorated with gigantic representations of the queen making offerings to Amon. The figure of the god has been consistently effaced—probably by Khuenaten—and roughly restored by Rameses II. The second and eastern door is much smaller, and leads to a part of the building entirely separate from the rest of the temple, and which I believe to have been specially dedicated to Thothmes I. It is entered through a covered vestibule with a single row of three columns running from north to south. A doorway in the vestibule leads into an open court, and in the midst of this court stands a great altar made of "good white An stone." The altar is dedicated to Harmakhis, and is so placed that the priest ascending the flight of steps leading to its platform would face the rising sun. Opposite the north side of the altar is a door leading to the little rock-cut chapel which I believe to be the funerary chapel of Thothmes I. Here we found the name of the king's mother—Senseneb. It is obvious, even from this brief description, that the north side of the upper platform considerably differs from the side cleared by Mariette, and that the two sides of the building are in no wise symmetrical to each other.

No chambers were built over the Northern Speos, nor yet over the Southern; and no use seems to have been made of the platforms above them, which were only intended to protect their roofs from the talus of the cliffs. I cleared the platform over the Northern Speos to the level of the pavement, and there found a panel of the ebony shrine dedicated by Thothmes II. This discovery led me to conclude that from the time of the destruction of the shrine, perhaps from the time of the reign of Khuenaten, rubbish and débris were allowed to accumulate on this spot, and that no one ever went there.

On the north side of the middle platform are the first columns of a colonnade starting from the Northern Speos, running from west to east, and having in its wall little niches for offerings such as are found elsewhere throughout the temple. In M. Brune's plan this is represented as a colonnade of thirty-seven columns, and as stretching the full length of the middle platform. Our excavations prove it to have been much shorter, and to have consisted of fifteen columns only.

CHAPTER IV.

THE FAMILY OF THE THOTHMES.

BEFORE considering the reign of the great queen who built the temple of Deir el Bahari, let us first investigate her family history. In this matter the conclusions of earlier Egyptologists have been successively modified by later discoveries. We will therefore explain the case as it now stands, though it is liable possibly to further important modifications from future research.

In the genealogical table of the XVIIIth Dynasty as drawn up by M. Maspero with the help of the inscriptions found on the Deir el Bahari mummies,[1] the wife of Amenophis I. is Queen Aahhotep II.; Thothmes I. being their son, and the princess Aahmes their daughter. Brother and sister married, and of that marriage was born Queen Hatshepsu, the founder of this temple. But Thothmes I. had two other wives : Mutnefert, whose son was Thothmes II., and Isis, evidently of inferior rank, whose son was Thothmes III. The genealogy which until quite recently seemed most likely to be correct ran as follows :

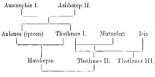

Hence Thothmes II. and Thothmes III. were both sons of Thothmes I., and consequently half

[1] *Mission archéologique française au Caire*, vol. i., p. 637.

[2] Maspero, *Proc. of the Soc. of Bibl. Arch.*, vol. xiv., p. 170.

brothers to Hatshepu, who became the wife of Thothmes II. and the guardian of Thothmes III.

An important alteration of this genealogical table was necessitated by M. Boussac's discovery of the great stela of Anna in a tomb at Goornah.[2] The stela tells us that "when king Thothmes II. appeared in heaven and rejoined the gods, his son took his place as king of the two lands, and he was prince upon the throne of him who begat him. His sister, the royal wife Hatshepsu, discharged the office of regent of the land." Thothmes III. is not here mentioned by name, but as there was no intermediate king between him and Thothmes II., Thothmes III. must needs have been the son of Thothmes II. This conclusion is confirmed from the dedicatory inscription of a statue at Karnak.

M. Maspero has therefore altered the second part of his genealogical table as follows :

In concluding his notice of the XVIIIth Dynasty, M. Maspero indicated one point as still doubtful. This first table makes Queen Aahhotep the mother of Thothmes I., and thus the king's wife Aahmes is his full sister. But M. Maspero did not consider this as conclusively settled, and we now find that his doubt is justified. Professor Erman has recently published an inscription on a piece of limestone in the Ghizeh Museum, which gives the text of a letter or circular sent round to his subordinates by Thothmes I. (in this instance to au officer at Elephantine), announcing his accession to the throne. In reference to the formula for oaths he says: [hieroglyphs] *Let them swear by the name of His Majesty, life, health, and strength, born of the royal mother, Senseneb.* From this inscription it would seem that Senseneb, although wife of Amenophis I., was not of royal blood, or that at any rate she had not been raised to the rank of queen. Now in the funerary chapel of Thothmes I. the king is represented with his well-known wife, the queen-sister Aahmes, [hieroglyphs] and also with another queen called *the royal mother, princess of the two lands, Senseneb,* who is evidently the one referred to in the Ghizeh inscription. This proves that Thothmes I. was only half-brother to his wife Aahmes. Senseneb is here called queen, and her name enclosed in a cartouche; but she is unmentioned in the royal genealogies, her elevation being probably due to her husband's favour. The amended genealogical table of the Thothmes family stands therefore as follows :

Aahhotep	Amenophis I.	Senseneb
Aahmes	Thothmes I.	Mutnefert
Hatshepsu	Thothmes II.	Isis
Hatshepsu II.	Thothmes III.

We here see that these four kings all married their half-sisters, a custom which lasted into Ptolemaic times, and which must have been founded on very ancient tradition. It is certainly the remains of what is known as endogamy, *i.e.,* marriage between the members of the family, and implies polygamy on the part of the father of the man and wife, the father having been the king in the cases now under consideration.

The mother of Thothmes III. was made known to us from the linen wrappings inscribed with texts from the Book of the Dead which enfolded his mummy. Immediately following on the title of Chapter I. are these words, [hieroglyphs] *Said by the king Menkheperra, son of the Sun, Thothmes, justified, son of the royal mother Isis, justified.* The name of Isis is not enclosed in a cartouche, and she has no other title than that of " royal mother "—*i.e.,* mother of a king. Hence we may infer that Thothmes II. had not raised Isis to the rank of queen, and that she was merely one of the royal harem. This fact may perhaps furnish us with the key to a problem which has never been satisfactorily solved, namely, that presented by the relations which subsisted between Hatshepsu and Thothmes III. Hatshepsu was the legitimate wife of Thothmes II., and seems to have had no son, but only two daughters, one of whom was her namesake. The son of Thothmes II., Thothmes III., was born of another wife, who was perhaps a rival or a slave ; and if Hatshepsu shared her throne with the only heir of Thothmes II., it was doubtless because she was constrained to do so either by circumstances or by custom, and not from any affection which she bore to her husband's son who was also her own nephew. The relations between aunt and nephew were certainly not characterised by attachment and mutual confidence, for with Thothmes III. they left no trace of anything but resentment, which he sought to appease by doing his utmost to destroy everything recalling the reign of Hatshepsu. It is the story of Sarah and Hagar as enacted in a royal family ; but the queen was less happy than the Sarah of Scripture, for she was obliged to instal Ishmael in the heritage of Abraham, to associate him with herself, and to give him her own daughter in marriage.

CHAPTER V.

HATSHEPSU.

LET us now consider the life of this queen in greater detail. Judging from her monuments we conclude that she did not fall below the standard of the rest of the XVIIIth Dynasty, certainly one of the greatest and most powerful of all the Egyptian dynasties. Ramaka,[1] Hat-shepsu, Numt Amen (pl. xiii.) was, as we have seen, the daughter of Thothmes I. (pl. xii.) and of his half-sister Aahmes (pl. xi.). She would seem to have given early evidence of her capacity to reign, for her father, Thothmes I., associated her with himself in the exercise of the sovereignty. A scene on one of the pylons at Karnak represents the king holding baton and mace, standing before a sanctuary containing the Theban triad, and preferring his request. In the accompanying inscription, and more especially addressing the god Amon, he says: " *I have come unto thee, king of the gods, I prostrate myself* (before thee). *In return for what I have done for thee do thou bestow Egypt and the Red Land* (the desert) *on my daughter Ramaka, living eternally, as thou hast done for me.*" Further on he proceeds to say : " *My daughter Usertkau* (one of her titles), *who loves thee, who is united unto thee,* (who is) *beloved, thou hast transmitted the world unto her,* (*thou hast united it*) *in her hands, thou hast chosen her as queen.*" That Thothmes I. voluntarily associated his daughter with himself upon the throne is proved from the fact that this inscription was engraved during his lifetime; had there been no other

record of his action in the matter than that engraved by order of Hatshepsu, and in her own temple, there might have been doubt on this point.

A fuller account of Hatshepsu's accession to the throne as co-regnant with her father is given in an inscription which I found last spring in the northern half of the temple, on the retaining wall of the middle colonnade, *i.e.*, on a place corresponding to that occupied in the southern half of the temple by the record of the Expedition to Punt. The inscription is somewhat obscure and requires close study. It can only be copied with great difficulty, because it has been chiselled over from end to end, like all inscriptions exclusively commemorating Hatshepsu, which Thothmes III. could not appropriate to himself as he appropriated the record of the Expedition to Punt.

Immediately preceding it are scenes referring to the birth of Hatshepsu and to her being suckled by the divine cow. These scenes are almost identical with those relating to the birth of Amenophis III. which adorn the walls of a chamber in the temple of Luxor, and were probably suggested by the representations at Deir el Bahari. The story of Hatshepsu's childhood is followed by the account of her enthronement, and this direct sequence implies that she was still very young when that event took place. From childhood, Hatshepsu is always represented in full male costume. In the Southern Specs she is depicted in the likeness of a boy being suckled by the Cow Hathor; she is shown as a youth in the scene which we are about to consider, and elsewhere throughout the temple of Deir el Bahari

---

[1] The transcription of the name of Amenophis III. in the tablets of Tell el Amarna shows that the correct reading of this cartouche must be *Ka ma ra.*

she appears as a full-grown man (pl. xiii.). Excepting as a goddess, she is never once represented under the form of a woman. She officiates as priest, and not as priestess; and when enthroned within a sanctuary she wears the head-dress of Osiris or of some other god,—even the beard is not omitted.

The enthronement inscription is accompanied by a scene illustrating the text, and finely carved in relief, like all the sculptures on this wall. Thothmes is seated within a shrine, his names and titles being inscribed above his head, and neither the figure of the king, nor his titles, nor the opening words of the text have been defaced. But it is otherwise with the rest of the scene and record. Thothmes holds by the left arm a young man, who is standing. This is the queen, whose names and titles are also placed above her head; and although inscription as well as figure have been hammered out, it is still possible to decipher the characters. The long text is hard to read, and at present I can only give a summary of it. It is at least evident that the king has summoned together the nobles of his kingdom, and tells them that he has conferred the prerogatives and insignia of royalty upon his daughter, whom they are henceforward to obey. A curious indication that this inscription was engraved by order of the queen, and not by order of Thothmes, is that he speaks of the queen in the masculine : ⌡⌐⌐⌐ 𓋴 𓂋 𓏠 literally, *The Majesty of him my daughter*, or 𓋴 𓂋 𓏠 *he, my daughter*. The inscription also contains a somewhat obscure allusion to the death of the king, followed by an account of the rejoicings which celebrated the accession of the queen. On that occasion her names and titles are said to be completed, *i.e.*, her two cartouches are henceforth preceded and followed by long formulas of epithets and attributes. At this time also there would seem to have been a reform of the calendar. The 1st of Thoth (which is the first day of the first month of the vague year) and the beginning of the

seasons (*i.e.*, the beginning of the fixed year which was founded upon the recurrence of certain natural phenomena—especially the rise of the Nile) were made to fall upon the same day, so the inscription tells us. From time to time the Ancient Egyptians must have felt the inconvenience noted in the Canopic inscription, that, namely, of finding such of their festivals as were regulated by dates in the vague year gradually making the round of the seasons. This was obviated by again causing the two years to begin on the same day. There was a fresh start; and since the difference between the two years was but that of one day in four years, the old inconvenience was unfelt during the reign of the prince who made the reform, and his successors were free to employ the same means as he had done when the disparity between the vague and fixed years became so great as to be troublesome.

Although the genealogy of the Thothmes kings from Amenophis I. to Thothmes III. can now be restored with almost absolute certainty, there is no such certainty with regard to the reigns, regencies, and co-regencies of the family. That Thothmes I. was the son of Amenophis I., and that he associated his daughter with himself upon the throne, are two well established facts. Mariette concluded from the inscriptions on an unpublished monument that Thothmes I. and Thothmes II. were for a time co-regnant. This seems to me altogether unlikely. Hatshepsu was not married when she joined her father on the throne, and if Thothmes I. and Thothmes II. reigned together, Thothmes I. must have associated his son as well as his daughter with himself—a most improbable proceeding. It would rather seem as though Hatshepsu had reigned alone in the interval between her father's death and her marriage with Thothmes II., and that it was during her sole reign that she founded the temple of Deir el Bahari. As a proof that the temple was not founded in the lifetime of Thothmes I., Mariette states that never once throughout the building is that king's legend found as the legend of a living sovereign. Although agreeing with Mariette's conclusion, I cannot support this statement. In a part of the temple which Mariette did not excavate, Thothmes I. does bear the titles of a reigning king. On an outer wall of the upper platform there is a long inscription, of which unfortunately only a small portion remains, but it undoubtedly refers to Thothmes I. as living.

Raaakheperka, worshipper of Amon, lord of the thrones of the two lands, beloved, giving life like the Sun eternally. This is certainly not the legend of a deceased king ; but oddly enough the inscription is a palimpsest. It is carved with hollowed out signs, while the rest of the sculptures are in relief, and traces of the older inscription which it superseded may still be discerned beneath it. Moreover, since it is inscribed on the outside of a wall of the funerary chapel of Thothmes I., I am inclined to think that it was a later addition made with the intention of attributing that building to him and not to his daughter.

Neither are the king's titles in the enthronement inscription those of a dead sovereign ; but this text was very likely engraved by the queen's orders, and may have been intended to settle the disputed legitimacy of her accession. In inscribing the walls of her temple with the long text illustrated by a scene representing Thothmes I. in the act of placing his hands upon her, she put herself as it were under his protection, and appealed to his authority in order to secure from her subjects the obedience which he himself had commanded them to give her. She succeeded in securing it during her life, but after she was dead her name was not admitted on the lists of legitimate sovereigns. Therefore, in spite of appearances, and notwithstanding the two inscriptions which seem to prove the contrary, I do not think that the temple of Deir el Bahari was consecrated in the life-time of Thothmes I.

Nor do I agree with Mariette in ascribing the erection of the two largest obelisks in Egypt, the obelisks of Hatshepsu at Karnak, to the joint reign of father and daughter. Unfortunately only one obelisk of this pair stands intact, while the second is in fragments, of which some may be seen serving as millstones in the neighbourhood of Thebes.

These obelisks were erected in the peristyle which precedes the great Hypostyle Hall. The inscriptions engraved on each of the four faces were intended to be in three lines on each face, and of the three lines the middle one is the most important. The side lines contain scenes of offerings made by different kings ; they are incomplete, but they represent Hatshepsu, Thothmes I., and even Thothmes III., a fact which proves that in part at least they were engraved after the queen's death. On all four sides the middle inscription only is complete.

The four great central texts are very important, and contain particulars upon which new light is thrown by the inscriptions of Deir el Bahari. On the north face we read : " Her Majesty caused the name of her father to be established on this monument, which was placed when the king of Upper and Lower Egypt, the king Raaakheperka, gave praise to the Majesty of this god. Her Majesty raised the two great obelisks on her first anniversary, for it was said by the king of the gods to thy father the king of Upper and Lower Egypt, Raaakheperka, Give orders that obelisks may be raised, and thy Majesty will complete this monument."

At first sight the text seems somewhat confused, and the difficulty of understanding it is increased by that change of persons from third to second which is common in Egyptian texts. According to this inscription it was Thothmes I. who had originally intended to erect the obelisks, and at the command of the god Amon ; but since the obelisks in question are here referred to in the plural and not in the dual, the divine command must have related to more than two. Thothmes I. obeyed, and began the work. He erected two obelisks in the vestibule

c

preceding that of the queen and immediately contiguous to the Hypostyle Hall.[1] One of these obelisks is still standing, and its inscriptions name him as sole king, without any mention of his daughter as co-regnant with him. These obelisks must therefore date from before the joint reign of Thothmes I. and Hatshepsu. The king was afterwards desirous of completing his undertaking, but he probably died either before or immediately after beginning to do so, for the obelisk raised by his daughter bears no other mention of him except in the scenes of offerings and in the inscription on the plinth, where he is qualified as ⟨hieroglyph⟩ i.e., as deceased. Hence the completion of the work of Thothmes I. by the erection of the two above-mentioned obelisks which bear the queen's name must be attributed to the sole reign of the queen. The queen was very proud of her work, and described it at length in the inscription on the plinth of the one which is still standing:—" I who sit in the palace remember who hath made me ; my heart hath hastened to make for him two obelisks of *smu* metal, whose tops reach unto the sky in the august hall of columns which is between the two great pylons of the king Ra-aa-kheper-ka (Thothmes I.) . . . the words of men now living. When they see my monument in the course of years, and see what I have done, beware of saying: I know not, I know not. This hath been done by covering the stone with gold all over. It is thus that it hath been done. I swear it by the love of Ra and the favour of my father Amon, who invigorateth my nostrils with life and strength."[2] In stating the length of time occupied by the work, this same text supplies data from which a very interesting fact may be deduced. The text says: " My Majesty began to work at this in the 15th year, and the first day of Mechir, till the 16th year, and the last day of Mesori, making

seven months since the beginning of it in the mountain." Here is incontrovertible proof that the regnal years of a sovereign were counted from the date of accession or coronation, and not from the 1st of Thoth. For, since Mechir was the second month of the second season, and Mesori the fourth month of the third, the seven months would necessarily have fallen in the same regnal year had that year been reckoned from the 1st of Thoth.

There is a remarkable agreement, in the matter of dates, between the obelisk inscription and the inscriptions at Deir el Bahari. According to these statements the erection of the obelisks in the temple of Karnak, and of Hatshepsu's building on the other side of the river, alike commemorated an anniversary of the queen's coronation. On the obelisk we read ⟨hieroglyphs⟩ *she has celebrated in his honour* (that of Amon) *the first anniversary of the Sed festival.* And again ⟨hieroglyphs⟩ *the two great obelisks were erected by Her Majesty at the first anniversary.* Now one of the most frequently recurring names of the temple of Deir el Bahari is that of ⟨hieroglyphs⟩ *the sacred place of the first anniversary.* In one of the inscriptions which I found, the god Amon speaks as follows : *Enter in peace, my daughter, within this good, and sacred, and pleasant place which thou hast made for me,* ⟨hieroglyphs⟩ *within the sacred place of the first anniversary.* The pillars of the colonnades repeatedly mention the Sed festival. In one of my former works I have described the celebration of a Sed festival at some length.[3] The general character of the festival is well known ; there is no doubt that it commemorated the sovereign's accession ; but the period of time which must

[1] Lepsius, *Denkm.*, iii. 6.
[2] Translation by Mr. Le Page Renouf, in *Records of the Past*, vol. xii., p. 131.

[3] *The Festival Hall of Osorkon II. in the Great Temple of Bubastis.*

have elapsed between a coronation and accession and the celebration of the Sed festival, and must again have elapsed before the sovereign was entitled to a second celebration of the same is not as yet determined. On the evidence of Ptolemaic inscriptions this period was first thought to have been one of thirty years—τριακονταετηρίς; but that conclusion is not borne out by the older instances, nor is it in accordance with the circumstances of the Sed festival with which we are now concerned. The festival to which reference is made in the inscriptions of Hatshepsu at Deir el Bahari must have been held at the laying of the first stone of the building, or else at its inauguration, when the obelisks were in place and the whole work completed; but even the second hypothesis gives the sixteenth, and by no means the thirtieth year of the queen's reign as the date of the celebration. Moreover, we have as yet no inscriptions of Hatshepsu later than the sixteenth year of her reign, which was also probably its limit. Hence there is here no question of a period of thirty years, of a τριακονταετηρίς; it is even improbable that the festival should not have been celebrated until towards the end of the reign, and from the Deir el Bahari inscriptions I should rather conclude that it was solemnised in the ninth year.

Besides the name commemorating the date of its foundation, the temple of Deir el Bahari more frequently bore that of ⏛⏛, ⏛⏛, serui, or serui Amon, the sacred place, or the sacred place of Amon. In this name there is nothing distinctive, the epithet ser being commonly applied either to persons, offerings, festivals, or places, i.e., to anything consecrated to divine use. It may be translated sacred, or worthy to be had in reverence.

We know the name of the architect to whose abilities Hatshepsu had recourse, and who probably superintended the building of the temple. In the museum of Berlin,[1] there is a statue of an official

called Senmut, who lived in the queen's reign. The numerous titles ascribed to him in its inscription are nearly all connected with buildings and the administration of estates. In accordance with the queen's usual practice, the inscription mentions her sometimes in the masculine and sometimes in the feminine. Senmut says: "I was a great man who loved his lord, and I gained the favour of my queen. He exalted me before the face of the land to the rank of overseer of his house, and purveyor of the land. I was chief over the chiefs, head of the architects,[2] I executed his orders in the land—I lived under the lady of the land, queen Ramaka, living eternally." His memory is perpetuated also upon the walls of his temple; in the Southern Speos his name occurs as worshipping Hathor.[3] The base of a squatting statuette of this great personage in black granite, and a broken glass bead inscribed with his name were found in the course of our recent excavations.

Is it to the queen or to her architect that the honour of inaugurating a new style of architecture —that of a temple wholly or in part rock-cut, and known as a speos or hemi-speos—is due? This style of temple developed greatly under Rameses II., and especially in Nubia; but we have no older examples of it than such as date from the XVIIIth Dynasty and the reign of Hatshepsu. There can be no doubt that the conception of the rock-cut temple of Deir el Bahari was suggested by the tombs of Beni Hassan. At Deir el Bahari as at Beni Hassan we find the square pillars, and more especially the characteristic sixteen-sided columns known as Proto-Doric, supporting architraves on square abaci not wider than the diameter of the columns, and without the echinus never omitted between the shaft and abacus of the Doric column. The Speos of Hathor further recalls the tombs of Beni Hassan

[1] Lepsius, Denkm., iii. 25.

[2] Duemichen, Hist. Insch., ii., pl. 31.

in its arrangement. I should think that Beni Hassan was the place where the queen made her first experiment in such architecture; for close to those tombs, in the valley known as Stabl Antar, she began the excavation of a speos which she never finished; but she completed both the lateral rock-cut sanctuaries of Deir el Bahari—that of the south or the Speos of Hathor, and that of the north, which I shall call the Speos of Anubis. These sanctuaries are symmetrically placed at either end of the middle colonnade.

The Speos of Hathor was certainly built before the Northern Speos, and dates from the time when Hatshepsu had ceased to reign alone, had married her brother Thothmes II., and was reigning together with him for a few years. Strictly speaking it is a hemi-speos. It is preceded by a covered colonnade, whose roof of enormous blocks rests upon Proto-Doric columns and four pillars with Hathor-head capitals. This forms the approach to a small hypostyle hall, hewn out of the solid rock and upheld by two Proto-Doric columns only, which leads into two narrow chambers, of which the further is the narrower and also the less lofty, owing to the rise in the floor. Here we find conformity to the same law which prevails in the hypæthral temples and M. Perrot has named " the law of decreasing dimensions": i.e., from portico to sanctuary (called the *sekos* by M. Perrot, and by others the *cella*) the dimensions of the building decrease in every sense and the floor itself rises. The innermost room contained the sacred emblem of the goddess, probably in the form of a cow made of gold or some other precious metal; and as usual in Egyptian temples the figure would be kept in a tabernacle or shrine. The sacred bark which bore the tabernacle containing

the emblem was probably kept in the room immediately preceding the sanctuary. The various lateral niches were the equivalents of the store chambers, built round the sanctuary of a temple to serve as repositories for offerings, precious things, the divine vestments, and all the sacred furniture.

It is interesting to compare the Southern Speos of Deir el Bahari with that of Rameses II. at Abu Simbel, also dedicated to the goddess Hathor. At Abu Simbel, as in most of the Nubian temples, the *sekos* is not blank, but on the inner wall is carved the forepart of the sacred cow represented as emerging from the mountain ; beneath her head is the figure of the king. A similar group is sculptured on the side-walls of the speos of Deir el Bahari. Hathor was pre-eminently the goddess of the mountain; she it was who emerged from the Mountain of the West, and to her the deceased made adoration. Nothing could have been more suitable to her character as set forth in the inscriptions than a rock-cut sanctuary hewn out of cliffs like those of Deir el Bahari, especially if that sanctuary were connected with a tomb. We cannot here pursue the comparison between the Egyptian rock-cut and hypæthral temples ; but each alike was intended as the dwelling-place of divinity, and in all its essential parts presented a close analogy with the Egyptian tomb destined for the dwelling of the dead. To judge from remaining monuments, Hatshepsu was the first to conceive the idea of applying the subterranean architecture hitherto confined to tombs to the requirements of divine worship : with her, or with her architect, originated the rock-cut temple in Egypt.

ONE of the most important events of Hatshepsu's reign was that naval expedition to the Land of Punt, whose sculptured record covers the southern half of the wall stretching behind the middle colonnade of her temple. The upper courses of the wall parallel to the colonnade are unfortunately in great part destroyed, and but little remains of the wall at right angles to it which closes in the colonnade on the south. A peculiar interest attaches to this expedition, since it was not one of conquest, but intended to establish commercial relations with peoples of the African coasts.

Whatever was the exact situation of the Land of Punt, it certainly belonged to what were known as the *lands of the South* 〰 . Did it also form part of the region called *Khent Hunnefer* a wide tract of country south of Egypt, stretching between the Nile and the Red Sea ? Brugsch holds that it did,[1] and bases his conclusion mainly upon the indubitable fact that in one of the great lists of Thothmes III. Punt appears under the general heading of peoples of the South and of Khent Hunnefer.[2] Nevertheless, Punt is generally distinguished from Khent Hunnefer, and particularly so in the inscriptions of Deir el Bahari, from which latter it would seem that the two countries were contiguous, but of somewhat wide and indefinite extent, Punt possessing a coast where vessels could put in, while Khent Hunnefer lay in the mountainous interior, and included the district of , which has been supposed to

be that of the Blemmyes. is read in several ways, of which M. Maspero's *Ilim* seems to me the most correct.

If Punt and Khent Hunnefer were not one and the same country, there was still great resemblance between them; each had a mixed population which included negroes, and their produce was almost identical.[3] On comparing the sculptures of Deir el Bahari with the somewhat later scenes from the tomb of Rekhmara, we see that in both cases incense is represented as the chief product of Punt, especially the kind called *anti*. The giraffe is said to come from Khent Hunnefer, and not from the coast. The dogs figured in the tomb of Rekhmara are brought from the interior, while those at Deir el Bahari come from Punt. Ivory, panther-skins, live panthers, gold, ebony, antimony, and various kinds of monkeys, were common to both countries. All these products being decidedly African, it is evident that Hatshepsu's expedition had been directed to an African coast, and that her ships anchored in an African port.

The arrangement of the Deir el Bahari sculptures, together with that of some of their accompanying texts, is obviously intended to convey the fact that the whole of the cargo and treasure was brought back by a single expedition, and not by two, of which one was maritime and the other overland, as some have supposed. " All these marvels," as the inscription calls them, were brought in the queen's ships from the one famous expedition which was her pride. And if products of the land of Ilim were among them, their pre-

---

[1] *Völkertafel*, p. 58.
[2] *Mariette, Karnak*, p. 22.

[3] *Hoskins, Travels in Ethiopia*, plates pp. 328-330.

sence only serves to show that commercial relations existed even then between the interior and the coast. The inhabitants of the hilly districts of Upper Nubia and the Soudan brought their native produce to Punt, whence it was passed on into other countries which had dealings with the people of that land. We should naturally conclude that the inhabitants of the coast had most frequent intercourse with their nearest neighbours, that is to say, with those peoples of Arabia separated from them by the Red Sea only. Classic writers, and particularly Herodotus[1] and Strabo,[2] speak of Araby the Blest and its wealth of divers perfumes. There lay the other shore, along which, as the inscription states, stretched the Land of Punt, or the Divine Land, 𓉿𓇌𓈗 for the two names seem to be synonymous. Hatshepsu's fleet undoubtedly sailed for the coasts of Africa and not for those of Arabia, but we are not justified in limiting the Land of Punt to the African coast alone. Punt, or Toneter, the home of perfumes dear to the Egyptians, and the land to which their religious texts ascribe an almost legendary character, lay upon both shores of the southern end of the Red Sea.[3] There, from remote antiquity, dwelt a trading population which exported incense, myrrh, cinnamon—all those perfumes for which ancient Orientals seem to have had a taste even more pronounced than that of their modern representatives, and which must also have been highly esteemed by the gods, since such large use was made of them in Egyptian ritual.

The five ships sent by the queen (pl. vii.) put in to shore in Africa, perhaps we can even approximately determine where; but, as M. Maspero[4] has pointed out (and I am of his

opinion in the matter), it was not on the coast. The sculptured scenes represent no coast scenery; such native huts, and trees tall enough to shelter the cattle, would not be found by the shore, nor do date-palms grow in the sand and pebbles of the beach. All this must have been at some distance inland, safe from the high tides of the Red Sea, and also out of the reach of ships. In order to anchor near the dwellings of the natives the Egyptians probably ascended one of the streams, wadys, or ποταμίαι noted by Greek geographers as frequent on this part of the coast, and which formed small natural harbours, identical in all likelihood with the "Harbours of Incense,"[5] as the inscription names the stations whence the perfumes and spices were brought. M. Maspero considers that the stream up which the Egyptians made their way was the "Elephant river," near to the mountain of that name and running between the Ras el Fil and Cape Guardafui, and his assumption is a plausible one. Still, it hardly seems necessary for the expedition to have gone so far south. The aromatifera regio began much nearer the Straits of Bab el Mandeb, near to the Gulf of Tajura; and according to Greek geographers the perfume and spice trade had many stations or ἐμπόρια all along this coast. We are unfortunately reduced to conjecture in the matter, for two-thirds of the short wall on which was sculptured the description of the Land of Punt is destroyed, and there is little hope of finding any of the scattered fragments which might yield invaluable geographical and ethnographical particulars.

The squadron having been made fast ashore, the queen's envoy, who has disembarked, is seen followed by an officer in command of eight soldiers armed with axe, lance, and shield

---

[1] III. 107.   [2] p. 778.

[3] Lieblein, Handel und Schiffahrt auf dem Rothen Meere, p. 52, et ff.

[4] De quelques navigations des Egyptiens sur les côtes de la mer Erythrée, p. 9, et ff.

[5] 𓊖𓉿𓂝𓏤 lit., the staircases or the ladders of anti, curiously corresponding to the French word échelle which in the East is applied to a harbour.

(pl. viii.). The presents from Egypt, that is to say such objects as the Egyptians had brought to offer in exchange for native produce, are placed upon a small table. The inscription of this scene says : " All good things " (from Egypt) " are brought by order of Her Majesty to Hathor, Lady of Punt." These presents consist of an axe, a poignard in its sheath, two leg bangles, eleven necklaces, and five large rings, which must have been wrought if they were made of precious metal, but, since gold was the product of the Land of Punt, I should rather suppose these rings to have been made of glass or glazed ware. Perhaps they were of bronze, or some other metal unknown to the natives. The poverty and meanness of the Egyptian gifts are in striking contrast to the value of those which they receive. In looking at this scene of barter we seem to be present at a transaction not unlike those which Europeans now make with negroes. The Egyptians presented their own manufactured goods, and the study of the scene has suggested to me that perhaps the necklaces, which here held the place of the beads of modern commerce, were made of scaraboids such as are commonly found at Deir el Bahari, whose chief beauty lies in the fine blue glaze which is characteristic of the ware of that place. The natives offered nothing but raw products ; no manufactured articles were then to be found among their gifts, any more than they are now included among their exports. At the most, the gold and precious metals were made up into rings.[1] The walls of Deir el Bahari probably show specimens only of what the Egyptians gave to the people of Punt, for the goods which the strangers are represented as taking away are out of all proportion to what they leave behind with the native chiefs, who, nevertheless, appear to have been well content with their bargain. It

is true that, as we see in the second row of scenes, in order to facilitate trade and secure native favour, a tent was set up and the chiefs were bidden to a feast of " bread, beer, wine, meat, fruits, and all the good things of Egypt, as the queen had commanded."

Distrusting the sight of armed men, the natives advance somewhat fearfully into the presence of the envoy, and speak with hands uplifted in supplication :—" How have you reached this land unknown to the men of Egypt? Have you descended hither by the paths of the sky, or have you sailed the sea of To-Neter ? " The native types and costume furnish an interesting subject of study, and Mariette concluded that the people were of two races. This may easily have been the case, since the trade of the interior came down to the coast-land of Punt, and we also know from the inscriptions that people of Hm came with the Puntites to greet the Egyptians. Individuals of the type to which the Prince of Punt belonged had aquiline noses, thick pendulous lips, and a hard expression of countenance. They grew long beards, curving outwards, and several of those distinguished as chiefs wore a feather in the hair, after the manner of some Libyan tribes. The group speaking with the envoy is that of the great chief and his family, and consists in the first place of the father, who is armed with nothing more than a boomerang and a poignard hanging from his belt. His right leg is protected by rings of yellow metal, forming such armour as the Bongo negroes wear on their arms, and to which they give the name of *dangabor*.[2] Behind him is his wife, who has dismounted from her ass. She is repulsively obese, her body being nothing but rolls and masses of flesh. She wears a yellow dress, and a necklace. The daughter is fast following in her mother's footsteps, and

---

[1] See these rings of precious metals being weighed in the scale after the return of the expedition. The weights are in the form of bulls.

[2] This is also true of the Niam Niam. Cf. Marno, *Reise in der Ægyptischen Æqualorial Provinz*, p. 124, where there is an illustration showing the figure of a chief wearing similar rings on leg, arms, and neck.

will in due time attain to the same proportions.[1] It was at first supposed that this monstrosity indicated some such disease as tuberculous leprosy, or elephantiasis; but African travellers, like Speke and Schweinfurth, state that among certain barbarous tribes of the interior such obesity is still the ideal of female loveliness. Speke recounts that in the case of one royal lady the weight of her arms alone prevented her standing upright. The Queen of Punt must certainly have found it difficult to enter her hut, which was built on piles, like the *tukuls* of some Soudanese tribes, and could only be reached by means of a ladder. 𓈝𓏤𓍼𓏺𓆓 *Parohu*, the name of the King, and 𓎟𓃾𓂋𓇌 *Ati*, that of his wife, have no ethnographical significance.

The type of the first group, which is also that of most of the population, is as well marked as that of the second is ill-defined; the latter being chiefly differentiated from the former by the absence of a beard and the presence of the round Egyptian wig. As neither type is represented with the characteristic colour and features of the negro, we must regard both types as belonging to Cushite or Hamitic race, akin to the Egyptian and probably of the same common origin.

The products of the Land of Punt carried away by the Egyptian ships were many and various. The inscription does not enumerate all those represented; *e.g.* it says nothing of the cattle and whether they came from Punt or the Land of Ilim. Cattle still constitute the chief wealth of many tribes on the Upper Nile, and travellers maintain that the Soudanese beasts are far superior to the Egyptian, a superiority doubtless already recognized in the reign of Hatshepsu. The text, however, duly records all the precious woods of To-Neter, and among

them the *Tashep*, which M. Loret has identified with the odoriferous cinnamon wood;[2] and the *Khesi*, which is as yet unidentified but was probably also odoriferous. But of all the woods which formed the staple timber trade, alike of Punt and of Khent Hunnefer on the Upper Nile, ebony held the chief place.[3] In the tomb of Ti we find reference to one of his statues as being of ebony. The wood is mentioned again and again from that time onward to the reign of Ptolemy Philadelphus, who made a troop of Ethiopians bearing two thousand trunks of ebony march in one of his processions. The Egyptians considered the bark good for the eyes, but the wood itself was in chief request for the manufacture of shrines, palettes, furniture and fine cabinetmaking, and works of art in general. Very likely the door and panel which I found in 1893, and which had formed part of a great shrine made for Amon during the joint reign of Hatshepsu and Thothmes II., is of Punt ebony.

The vegetable products of Punt in the greatest demand were spices and perfumes, of which the chief kinds were called 𓎟𓏤𓈖𓎛 cassia(?), 𓊃𓈖𓊮 incense, and above all 𓂋𓈖𓏏 *anti*, which was collected in lumps, like gum, and piled in large heaps. The trees which bore it were also exported; dug up while still young, they were set in wooden boxes of earth to be placed here and there in gardens as we put orange-trees (pl. x.), or to be transplanted into ground where they eventually grew tall enough for cattle to pass beneath them (pl. ix.). The *anti sycamores*, as these trees were called, have not yet been identified. Perhaps the bas-reliefs exaggerate their size, as is always the case where the possessions of a god or king are in question. As Amon and Pharoh were greater than ordinary mortals, so trees transplanted into the garden of Amon would

---

[1] Since the publication of Mariette's *Deir el Bahari*, both scenes containing the figure of the Queen of Punt have been cut out of the wall and stolen. The upper scene was recovered and is now in the Ghizeh Museum; the lower, which also contains the daughter's figure, has never been found.

[2] *La Flore Pharaonique*, p. 21.

[3] See M. Loret's remarkable article, "*L'ebine chez les anciens Egyptiens*," in the *Recueil de Travaux*, vi. p. 125.

attain to unusual size. But their name of syca-more, and the very shape of the young saplings, which seems to imply forest trees with thick trunks, tell against Mariette's supposition that they were myrrh trees, specimens of the *Balsamo-dendron myrrha*. Myrrh is the produce of a shrub which grows abundantly on the Somali coast and in Arabia, but never exceeds nine or ten feet in height ;[1] this shrub cannot be the tree repre-sented at Deir el Bahari. A late inscription[2] states that there were fourteen kinds of *anti*, eleven of which were derived from the sycamore and were probably different preparations of the same thing. *Anti* was not only used for religious purposes, but also as a drug.[3] The large quantity imported shows how extensively it was employed.

The sycamores were planted in the garden of Amon, and the queen evidently thought this a highly meritorious deed. As kings have been credited with the invention of industries at which their hands never laboured, so perhaps Hatshepsu, by not confining her bounties to the temples, may claim to have diffused throughout her kingdom the culture of the incense-bearing sycamore, which pros-pered in Egyptian soil and was a notable addition to the material wealth of her subjects. On the same wall as that which records the Expedition to Punt is an inscription of the queen's ninth year, in which we read :— [hieroglyphs] *he has pulled up the sycamores of To-Neter and placed them in the soil of* (Egypt). And again [hieroglyphs] *He* (Amon) *has pulled up the trees of To-Neter and has placed them in his dwelling, in his orchard, as Her Majesty hath commanded.*

After Hatshepsu, and on a far larger scale, Rameses III. also despatched an expedition to the Land of Punt. On its return with similar mer-chandise the king thus addressed Amon[4] : " I plant for thee incense-bearing sycamores within thy courts," adding :—" The like had not been seen since the time of Ra "—an entirely unvera-cious statement, for the trade in *anti* sycamores had been kept up from the time of Hatshepsu onwards, as may be seen from the wall-paintings in the tomb of Rekhmara, which date from the reign of Thothmes III.

We need not dwell on the other products depicted on the walls, such as ivory, &c. The panther-skins were chiefly used to make vestments for certain orders of priests. *Mestem* was in great request for applying as paint round the eyes, to increase their apparent size. Prof. Wiedemann has shown that this name was given to different substances, such as oxide of lead, superoxide of manganese, and even to antimony. But it invariably denotes a mineral substance of which great quantities were imported into Egypt from remote antiquity. Among the products of Punt represented as piled beneath the sycamores is one named [hieroglyphs] *Kash*, followed by a curious determinative (pl. ix.). It lies in three pieces, larger than the lumps of incense, and I take it to be so many tortoise shells,[5] articles which formed part of the trade of the *aromatifera regio*, according to the Periplus of the Erythraean Sea.[6] The gold qualified as [hieroglyph] —literally green or fresh,—and which came from the land of *Amu*, is probably gold in nuggets, or gold dust, as dis-tinguished from the gold which has been worked up into rings. As to the animals brought from Punt and Ilim—panthers, dogs, leopards, giraffes— we know that wealthy Egyptians always took pleasure in keeping live specimens of foreign fauna, and more especially monkeys, of which they regarded several kinds as sacred.

Such was Hatshepsu's Expedition to the Land of Punt, and one of the chief events of her reign.

---

[1] Woenig, *Die Pflanzen im Alten Aegypten*, p. 355.

[2] Duemichen, *Geog. Insch.*, ii. 86-88 and p. 66 of the text.

[3] Ebers Pap., *passim*.

[4] Harris Pap., pl. vii., l. 7.

[5] χελώνη. Turtles are represented as well as fishes in the water of the Red Sea (pl. viii.).

[6] *Perip.*, pp. 264, 265, ed. Müller.

CHAPTER VII.

END OF HATSHEPSU'S REIGN, THOTHMES II., AND THOTHMES III.

BESIDES undertaking the enterprise of despatch-
ing a large commercial expedition to the Land
of Punt, Hatshepsu found other work to her
hand. In a long inscription at Stabl Antar
she recounts the mighty deeds of her reign, and
says : " I restored what was in ruins, and I built
up again what had remained (incomplete) when
the Aamu were in the midst of Egypt of the
North, and in the city of Hawar, and when the
Shasu (Shepherds) among them had destroyed
the ancient works. They reigned ignoring Ra,
and disobeying his divine commands until I sat
down on the throne of Ra."[1] It is difficult not
to consider these words as applying to the ravages
of the Hyksos, whose dominion, though greatly
weakened by the wars waged against them by
the kings of the XVIIth and XVIIIth Dynasties,
was not altogether cast off until the time of
Thothmes III. I know that this view, held by
Lepsius, is not endorsed by M. Maspero ; yet the
fact remains that hitherto no single monument of
the XVIIIth Dynasty earlier than the reign of
Thothmes III. has been found in the Delta. If
this fact is noted in connection with the queen's
statement in the inscription of Stabl Antar—
after making all due allowance for the exaggeration
characteristic of such documents—we can hardly
fail to admit that peace cannot have been fully

restored to the eastern parts of the Delta, and
Pharaonic rule completely re-established there
before the time of Hatshepsu.

Little more is known of the events of her reign,
but it is evident that the queen displayed both
the energy and the ruling power which her father
must have discerned before associating her with
himself upon the throne. After his death she
probably reigned for some time alone. Unlike
Thothmes I., she was not chiefly concerned with
foreign conquest, but rather in improving the
internal condition of the country and restoring
order to the land ; the Expedition to Punt proves
that she tried to develop Egyptian trade. The
date of her marriage with her brother, Thothmes
II., is unknown ; he played clearly a very subor-
dinate part in the state. On buildings dating
from his reign his name is almost invariably
connected with that of Hatshepsu, both at Karnak
and at Deir el Bahari ; in the latter temple it is
chiefly found in the Southern Speos and in the
niches of the upper platform. He apparently
conducted a successful campaign against the
Shasu, and another in Nubia, as we learn from a
stela at Aswan dating from the second year of his
reign. The second campaign must have been the
more important, and it was during its course that
he erected a fort at Kummeh, above the second
cataract. His reign was short, and it is evident
from his mummy, now in the Ghizeh Museum, that

---

[1] Naville, *Bubastis*, p. 29.

he cannot have been much more than thirty years old when he died. His skin was white, and is marked with the effects of some cutaneous disease which may have been the cause of his death.[1]

Hatshepsu survived him, and was obliged to take her husband's son and her own nephew, Thothmes III., as her co-regent. I have already explained what I take to be the cause of the ill-feeling existing between aunt and nephew. This mutual antipathy has sometimes been attributed to a wrong source. Prof. Brugsch,[2] interpreting a mythological inscription as a piece of personal history, says that Thothmes was originally excluded from all share in the sovereignty, and that his aunt banished him to the marshes of Buto, where Isis was said to have hidden Horus in safety from Typhon, who had compassed the death of Osiris. MM. Maspero[3] and Meyer[4] have shown that this story is to be regarded as pure mythology, invented to create a belief in divine origin and an education like that received by the children of the gods. Here, as elsewhere, Thothmes has imitated Hatshepsu's account of herself. In an outer scene of the Speos of Hathor the divine cow is represented as licking the queen's hand and addressing her as follows: "I smell thy hand, I lick thy flesh, I grant unto thy Majesty life and prosperity, as I did unto Horus in the marshes of Kheb. I myself suckle thy Majesty!" Other Egyptian sovereigns have referred to their childhood in similar terms.

It is mainly in the sanctuary, i.e. in the rock-cut chamber in a line with the axis of the building, that we find evidence of the joint reign of Thothmes III. and Hatshepsu. Here the figures of king and queen may still be discerned, kneeling, and making wine and milk offerings to Amon;[5] but these scenes have been much defaced since the time of Lepsius. The queen of course takes precedence; behind her stands the king, and behind him the princess Neferura, who was probably intended to become his wife. She was the eldest daughter of Hatshepsu, and in prospect of the high station to which she was destined her mother had already provided her with a household establishment. Senmut, the famous architect who directed the construction of all the buildings raised by Hatshepsu, was also steward to Neferura, and when recording upon the rocks of Aswan how he had been sent to procure the obelisks according to the queen's command he does not omit to mention that he was attached to the service of the young princess.[6] In the account which an officer named Aahmes, buried at El Kab, has left of his long life lasting from the time of King Aahmes to that of Thothmes III., he states that he had found favour with the Queen Hatshepsu, and had brought up her eldest daughter Neferura.[7] Neferura never came to the throne; it was not she who became the mother of Amenophis II., but Hatshepsu-meri-Ra, usually known as Hatshepsu II., who, to judge by her name alone, must also have been the daughter of Hatshepsu, though we have no formal proof that it was so. It is noteworthy that the name of the wife of Thothmes III. has never been found in the temple of Deir el Bahari.

Thothmes III. effaced the name of his aunt and co-regent throughout the place, and also many of her portraits. Where he did not think it worth while to destroy the latter he replaced the accompanying cartouches by his own or those of Thothmes II., and thus effected an easy transformation, since the queen is always represented as a man, and in male attire. But when confronted by an inscription which he could not attribute to himself he ruthlessly effaced the

[1] Maspero, *Les momies royales de Deir el Bahari*, p. 547.
[2] *Gesch. Aegyptens*, p. 365.
[3] *Zeitschrift*, 1882, p. 133.
[4] *Gesch.*, p. 308.
[5] Lepsius, *Denkm.*, iii. 20.
[6] Lepsius, *Denkm.*, iii., 25 bis.
[7] Lepsius, *Denkm.*, iii. 43.

whole of it. His antipathy was, however, confined
to Hatshepsu alone and did not extend to her
family. He respected the memory of his grand-
father, Thothmes I., who was the father, and also
that of his great-aunt Aahmes, albeit she was the
mother of Hatshepsu. He even spared the figure
of the princess Nefernkheb, a daughter of Aahmes
and Thothmes I., and full sister of Hatshepsu,
but who never came to the throne. These facts
might suggest some doubt as to whether all the
destruction attributed to Thothmes III. should
really be laid to his charge. Setting aside
Khuenaten and his rage for doing away with
everything recalling the name and figure of
Amen, was there only Thothmes III. among
Hatshepsu's successors whose interest lay in con-
signing her memory to oblivion? Amenophis III.,
who plagiarised the whole record of the queen's
miraculous birth on the walls of his own
adjacent temple at Luxor, had he no inducement
to wipe out the marvellous story which showed that
he was not the first sovereign with the right to
glory in having the god himself for father?
These are hypotheses whose value excavation
may some day determine.

In conclusion, if we consider such monuments
of this queen as have been spared, and also the
short duration of her reign, we are constrained to
admit that although her rule may not have
equalled in splendour and in power that of her
great XIIth Dynasty predecessors, or that of the
mighty conquerors who succeeded her upon the
throne, Egypt must still have enjoyed years of
wealth and prosperity while the sceptre was
held by her somewhat despotic hand.

INDEX.

CONTENTS OF PLATES.

—•─•─•─•─

PLAN BY THE FRENCH EXPEDITION

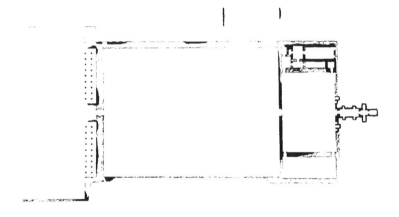

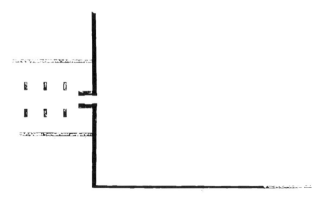

SPEOS DE L'OUEST

SPEOS DE SUD

TERRASSE DE L'OUEST

SPEOS DE NORD

TERRASSE DU CENTRE

PLAN BY MARIETTE.

TERRASSE DE L'EST

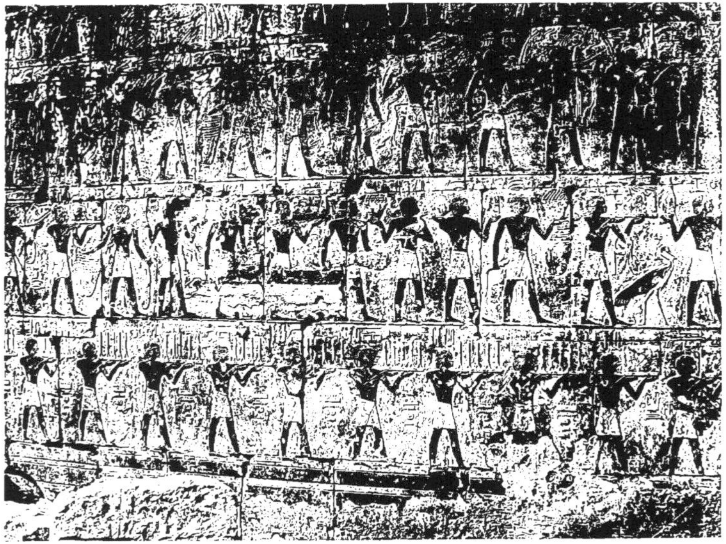

FUNERARY OFFERINGS TO THE QUEEN HATSHEPSU.

Plate V.

THE EXCAVATIONS IN JANUARY, 1894

SOUTHERN PART OF THE MIDDLE COLONNADE. WALL OF PUNT.

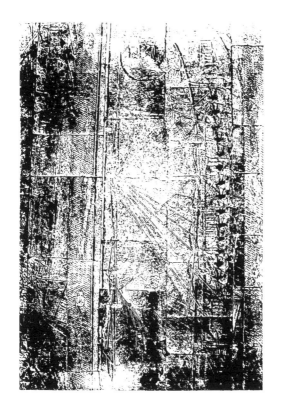

EXPEDITION TO PUNT. EGYPTIAN SHIPS LANDING AND SAILING OFF.

PLATE VIII.

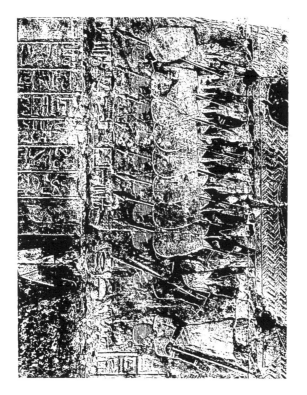

EXPEDITION TO PUNT. EGYPTIAN OFFICER AND SOLDIERS.

FRANKINCENSE TREES PLANTED IN AMON'S GARDEN.

WEIGHING THE PRECIOUS METALS.   FRANKINCENSE TREES IN POTS.

PLATE XI.

QUEEN AAHMES. HATSHEPSU'S MOTHER.

Plate XII.

KING THOTHMES I. HATSHEPSU'S FATHER.

.

PLATE XIII.

QUEEN HATSHEPSU IN MALE ATTIRE.

PLATE XIV.

HAWKS ON THE SUPPORTING WALL OF THE MIDDLE PLATFORM.

EGYPT EXPLORATION FUND PUBLICATIONS.

PUBLICATIONS OF THE ARCHÆOLOGICAL SURVEY OF EGYPT.

Edited by F. Ll. GRIFFITH, B.A., F.S.A.

Hon. Vice-President for America:
CHARLES DUDLEY WARNER, Esq., L.H.D., L.L.D.

Vice-President and Hon. Treasurer for America:
REV. W. C. WINSLOW, Ph.D., D.C.L., L.L.D., &c., Boston, Mass.

Druck:
Customized Business Services GmbH
im Auftrag der KNV-Gruppe
Ferdinand-Jühlke-Str. 7
99095 Erfurt